A FUN GUIDE TO FOOTBALL!

BY:

DEAMER K HOLDINGS

PLAYFUL PLANET KIDS SHOW

THIS BOOK BELONGS TO

PLAYFUL PLANET
KIDS SHOW

AI Disclaimer

Copyright

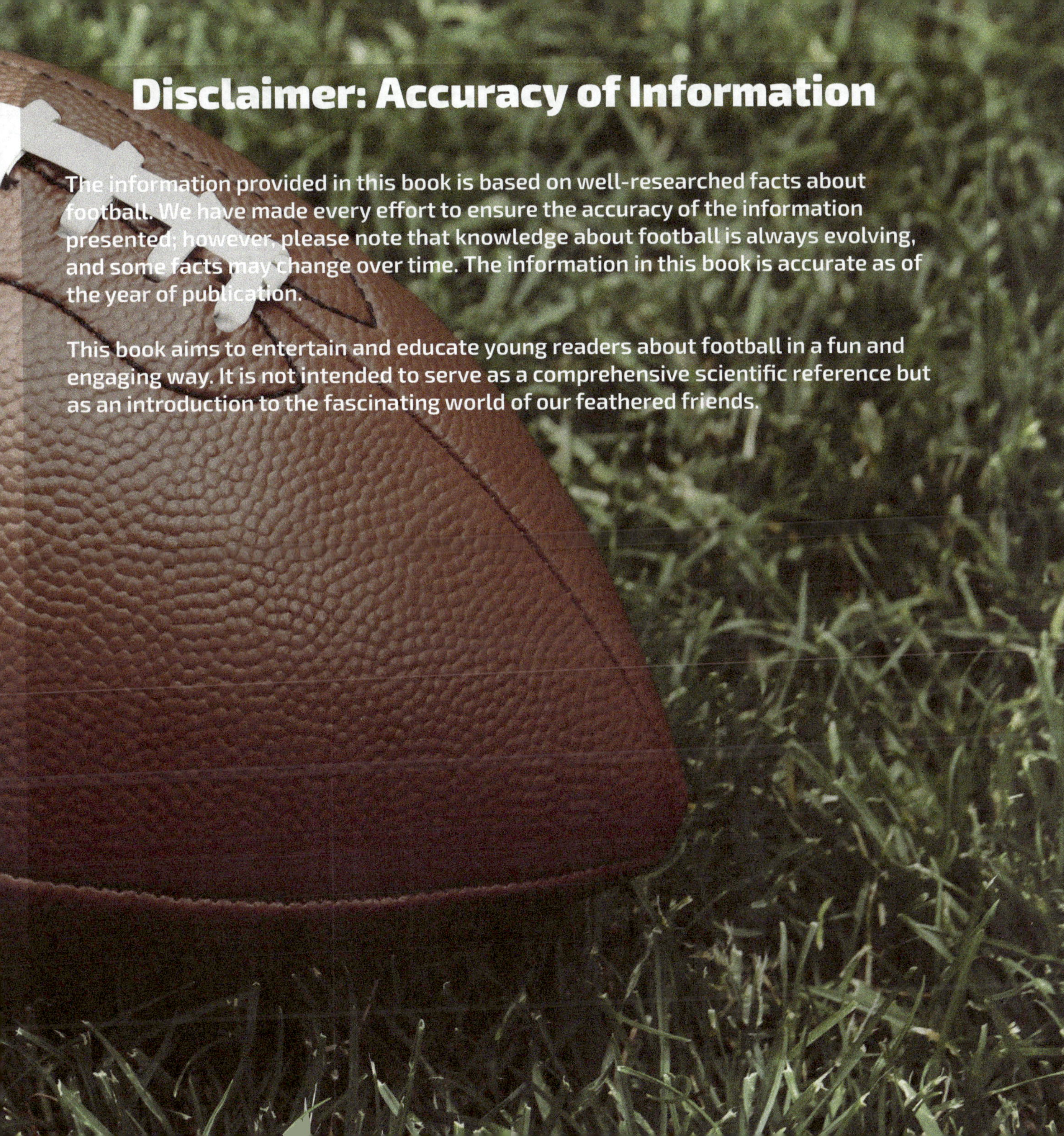

Disclaimer: Accuracy of Information

The information provided in this book is based on well-researched facts about football. We have made every effort to ensure the accuracy of the information presented; however, please note that knowledge about football is always evolving, and some facts may change over time. The information in this book is accurate as of the year of publication.

This book aims to entertain and educate young readers about football in a fun and engaging way. It is not intended to serve as a comprehensive scientific reference but as an introduction to the fascinating world of our feathered friends.

American football is an exciting and fast-paced sport played by millions of kids and adults across the country! Whether you want to play with friends, join a team, or just toss the ball around, football is a great way to stay active and have fun.

Football has a rich history that dates back to the late 19th century. It evolved from soccer and rugby, with the first official game played in 1869 between Rutgers and Princeton.

Over the years, the sport developed its own unique rules, positions, and strategies, shaping it into the game we know today. The National Football League (NFL), established in 1920, helped popularize football across America, making it one of the most beloved sports in the country.

In this book, you'll learn the rules of the game, how to play, where to play, what you need to get started, some of the most famous football players of all time, and cool strategies and moves you can try! Whether you're a beginner or already know a little about the sport, this guide will help you improve your skills and knowledge while having tons of fun on the field!

Chapter 1:

The Basics of American Football

Football is a team sport played between two teams of 11 players each. The goal is to score points by carrying or passing the ball into the opposing team's end zone. The team with the most points at the end of the game wins!

- **End Zones** – Where teams score touchdowns.

- **Yard Lines** – Marking every 5 yards on the field.

- **Goalposts** – For extra points and field goals.

- **The 50-Yard Line** – Center of the field.

- **Sidelines and Hash Marks** – For positioning the ball.

A Football Field Has:

Chapter 2:

How to Play

Football is played in four quarters, with each team trying to move the ball down the field to score.

1. **Kickoff** – The game starts with a kickoff, where one team kicks the ball to the other.

2. **Downs** – Each team has four chances (downs) to move the ball 10 yards. If they succeed, they get another four downs.

3. **Passing & Running** – The quarterback can throw the ball to a teammate or hand it off to a running back.

4. **Scoring:**

Touchdown (6 points) – Running or catching the ball in the end zone.

Extra Point (1 or 2 points) – Kicking the ball through the goalposts (1 point) or running/passing into the end zone (2 points).

Field Goal (3 points) – Kicking the ball through the goalposts from the field.

Safety (2 points) – Tackling an opponent in their own end zone.

Here's how it works:

Chapter 3:

The Rules of the Game
To play fair and have fun, here are some important rules:

What refs wear!

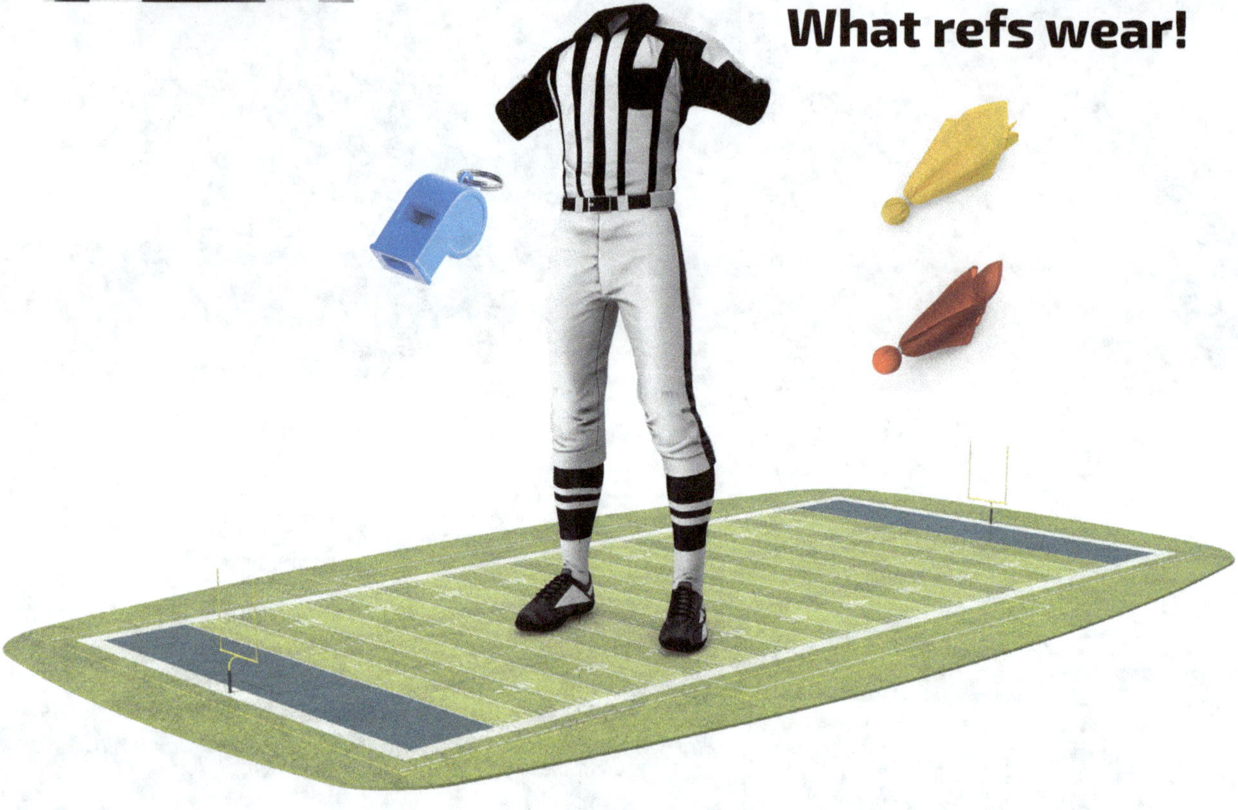

- **Each play starts with a snap** – The center passes the ball to the quarterback.

- **No tackling players without the ball** – Only the ball carrier can be tackled.

- **Fouls & Penalties:**

- **Offside** – Moving before the ball is snapped.

- **Holding** – Grabbing an opponent unfairly.

- **Pass Interference** – Blocking a receiver before they can catch the ball.

- **False Start** – An offensive player moving before the snap.

important rules to follow:

Chapter 4:

Where to Play
You can play football almost anywhere! Here are some common places:

- Backyards or open fields with friends.

- School playgrounds during recess or PE class.

- Community centers that offer youth leagues.

- Official football fields for organized games.

Stadium

A football field:

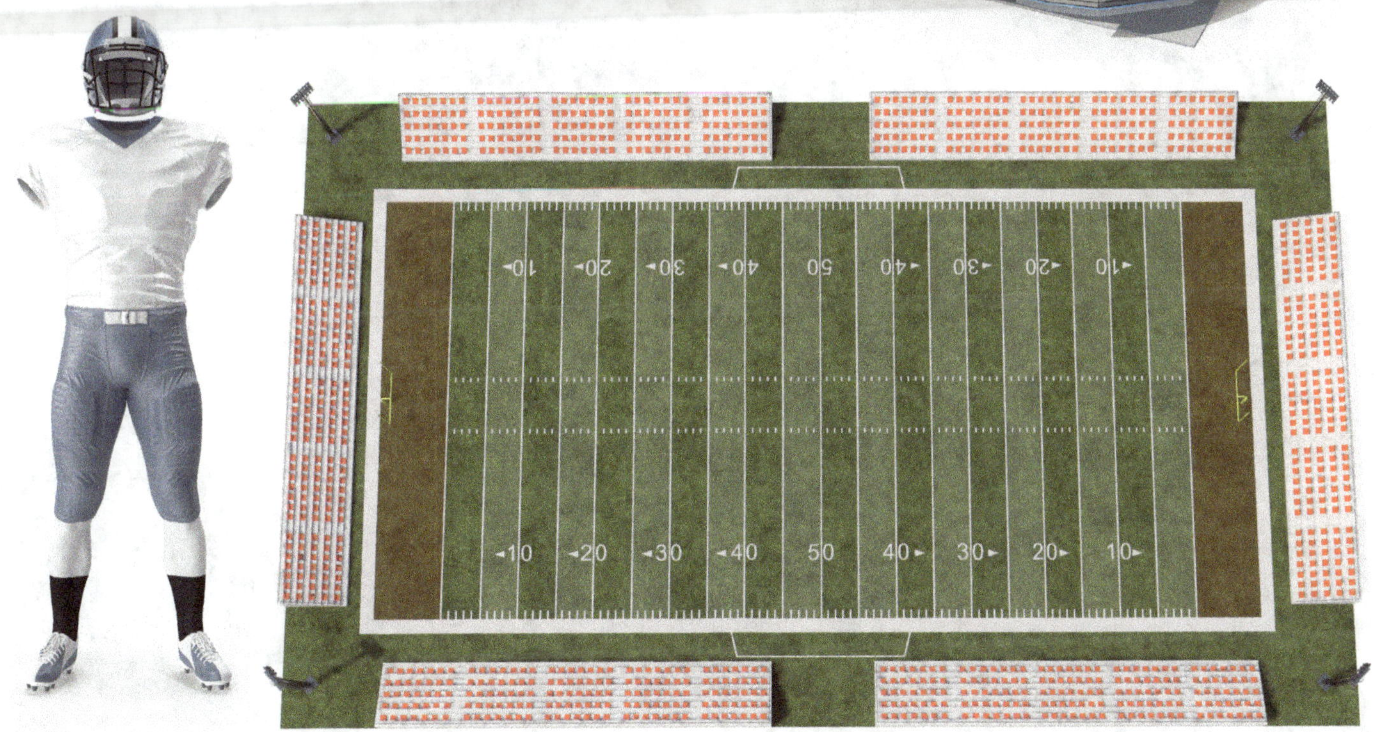

Chapter 5:

What You Need to Play

To start playing football, you only need a few things:

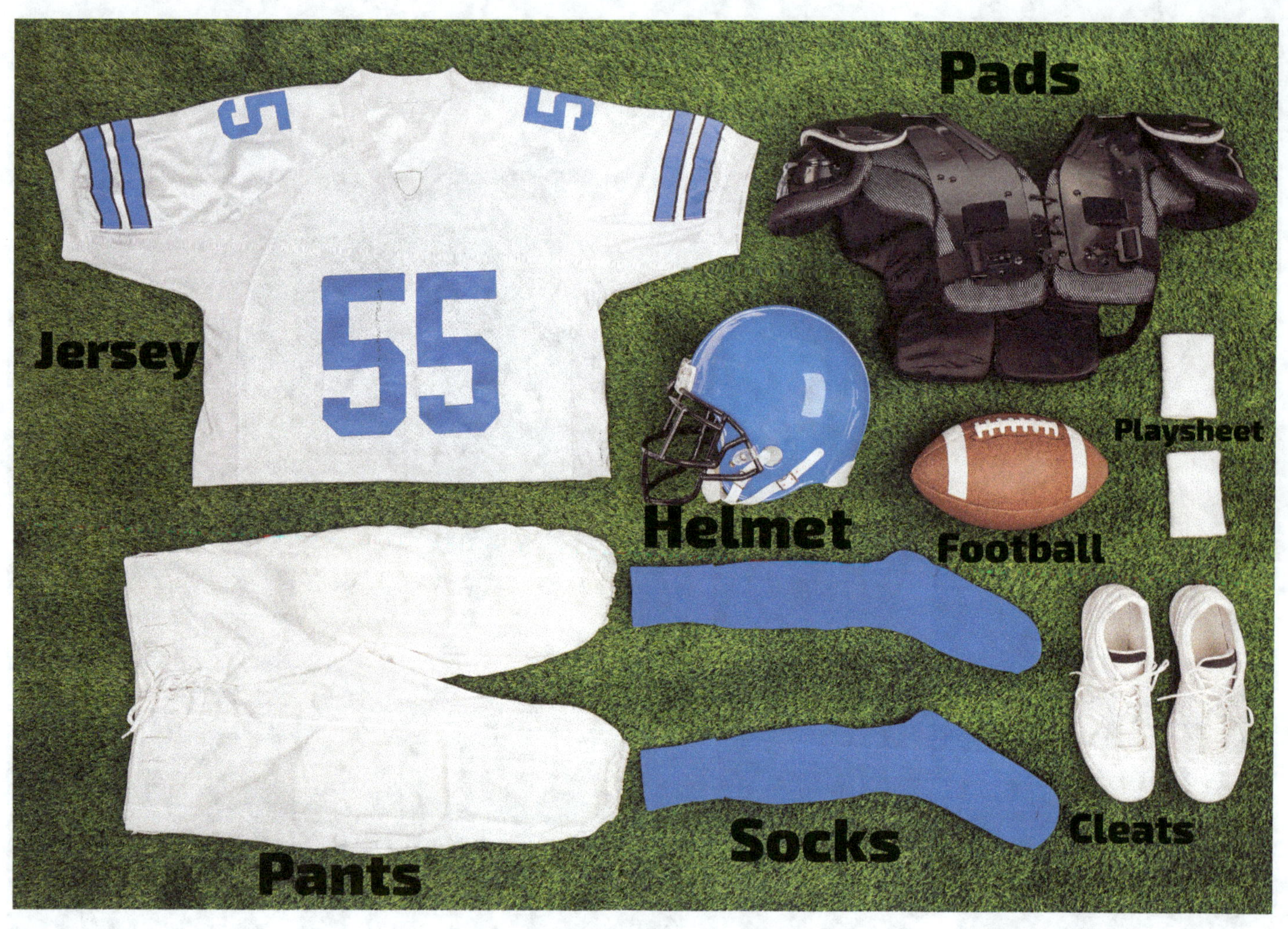

- A football (choose the right size for your age)

- A playing field

- Comfortable athletic clothes and cleats

- Optional: protective gear (helmet, shoulder pads, mouthguard)

- Friends or a team to play with!

A football game:

Helmet

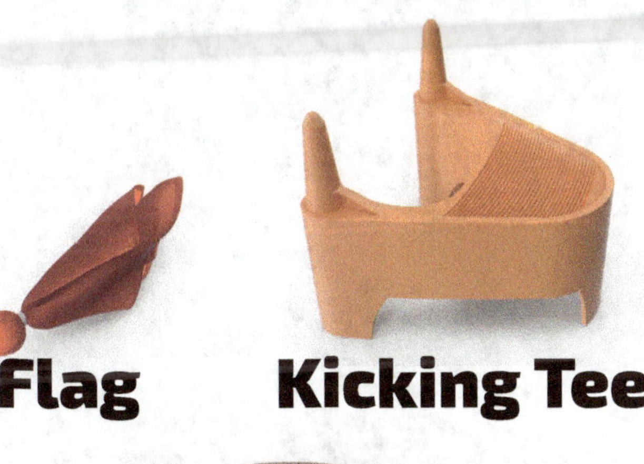

Pads

Cleats

Flag

Kicking Tee

Football

Chapter 6:

Basic Strategies and Cool Moves

To play better and impress your friends, here are some simple strategies and cool moves you can try:

Basic Strategies:

- **Offensive Playbook** – Running and passing plays to move the ball forward.
- **Defensive Formations** – Strategies to block passes, stop runners, or sack the quarterback.
- **Special Teams** – The unit responsible for kickoffs, punts, and field goals.

Cool Moves:

- **Spin Move** – Spinning to avoid a tackle.
- **Juke Move** – Faking one way and moving the other.
- **Hurdle** – Jumping over a defender.
- **Stiff Arm** – Using your arm to push a defender away.
- **Diving Catch** – Jumping forward to grab a pass.

Basic Strategies:

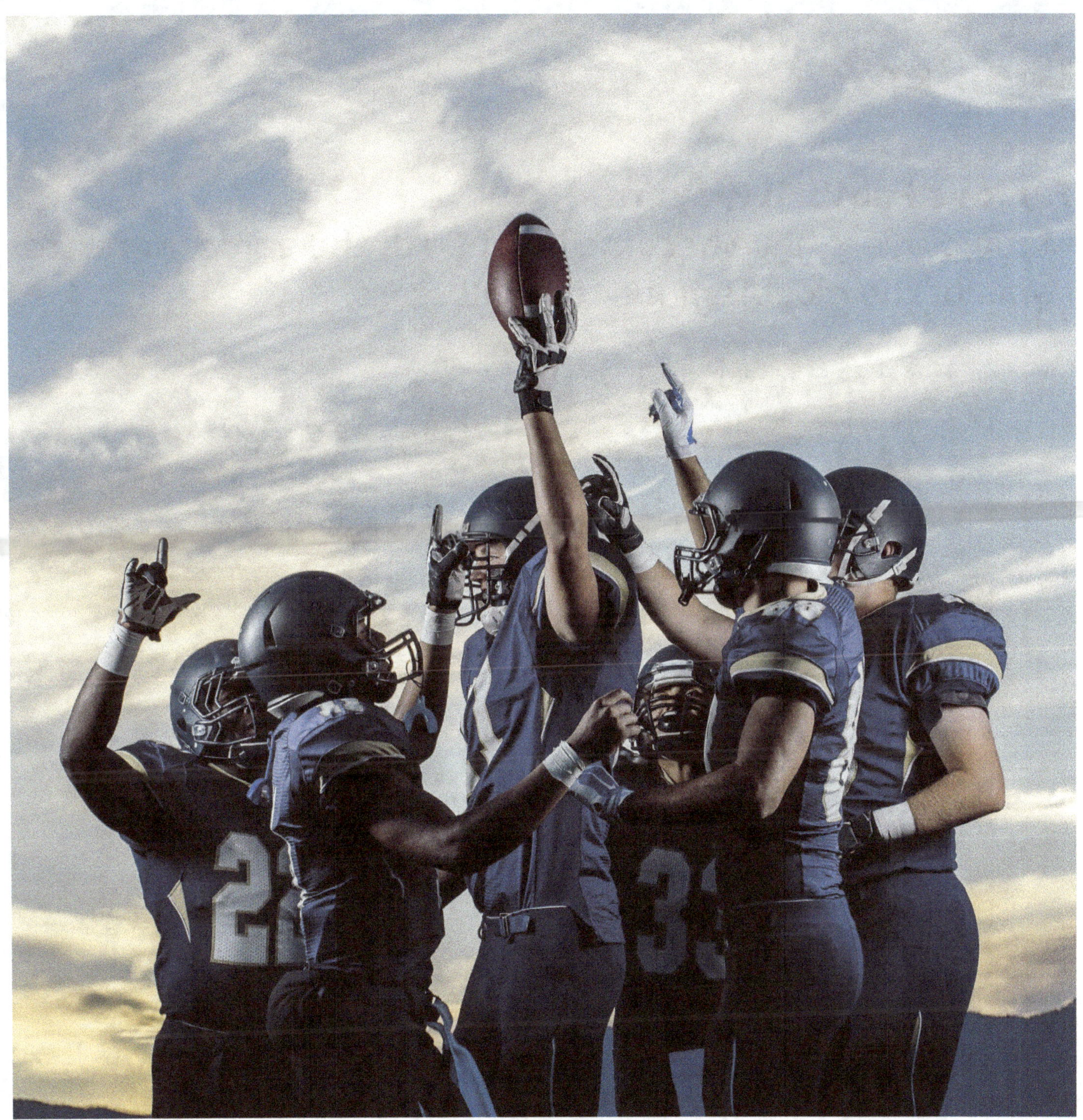

Chapter 7:

Famous Football Players

Many players have become legends of the game. Here are some of the most famous football stars:

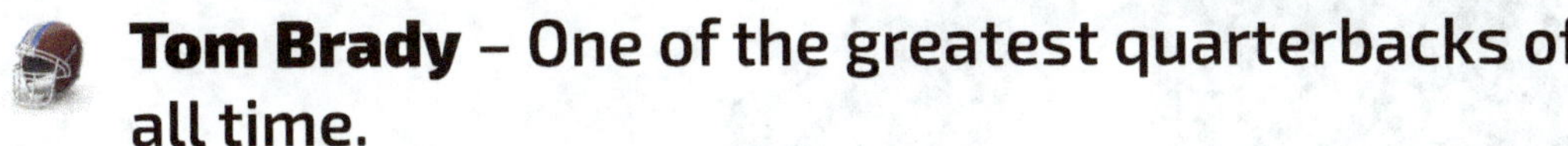 **Tom Brady** – One of the greatest quarterbacks of all time.

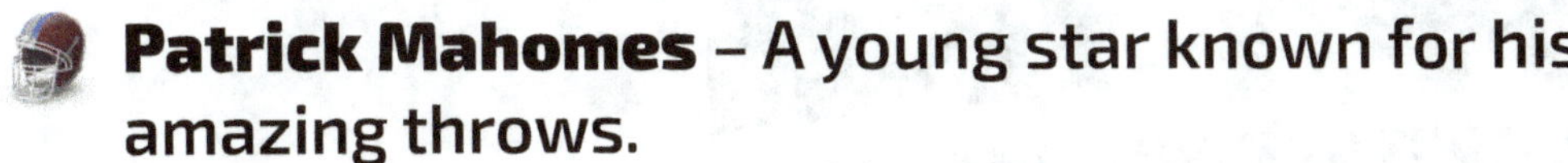 **Patrick Mahomes** – A young star known for his amazing throws.

 **Walter Payton** – A legendary running back with incredible moves.

Jerry Rice – The best wide receiver in history.

Jim Brown – One of the best women's basketball players, a pioneer in the WNBA.

Peyton Manning – A powerful running back from the early days of the NFL.

Doug Williams – the first black quarterback to both start and win a Super Bowl

Chapter 8

Age Group	Ball Size	Approximate Length	Circumference (Middle)	Common Use
Ages 6–9	Size 1 (Pee Wee)	10–10.5 inches	17.5 inches	Youth leagues, casual play
Ages 9–12	Size 2 (Junior)	11 inches	18.5 inches	Youth leagues
Ages 12–14	Size 3 (Youth)	11–11.25 inches	19.25 inches	Middle school
Ages 14+ (High School–College)	Size 4 (Official)	11.25–11.5 inches	21 inches	High school, college
NFL (Pro)	Size 5 (Pro/NFL)	11.5 inches	22 inches	Professional NFL games

Goalpost Dimensions

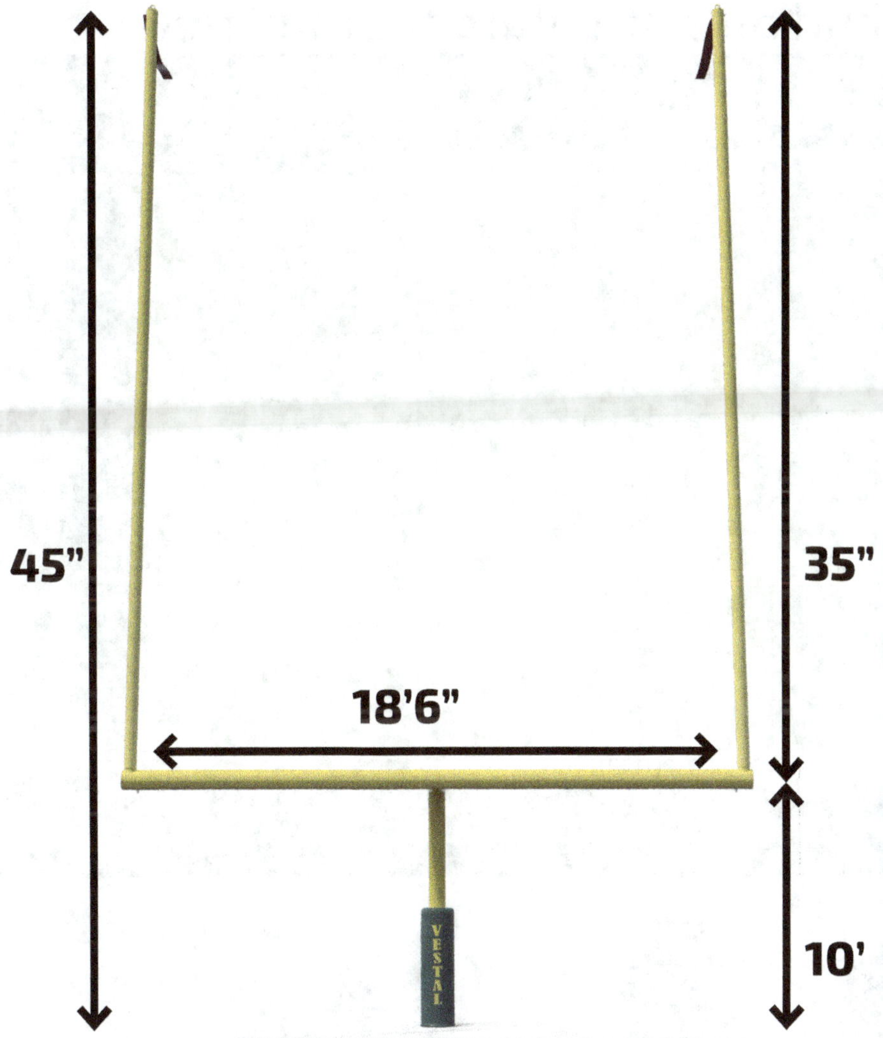

Goalpost
- Crossbar height: 10 feet above the ground

- Upright posts: Extend 35 feet high (or higher) from the crossbar

- Width between uprights: 18 feet, 6 inches

Kickers aim to get the football between the uprights and over the crossbar to score!

Football Field Dimensions

- A football field is big—it's the size of about 1 1/3 soccer fields or more than 100 basketball courts lined up! Here's what you'll find on a standard football field:

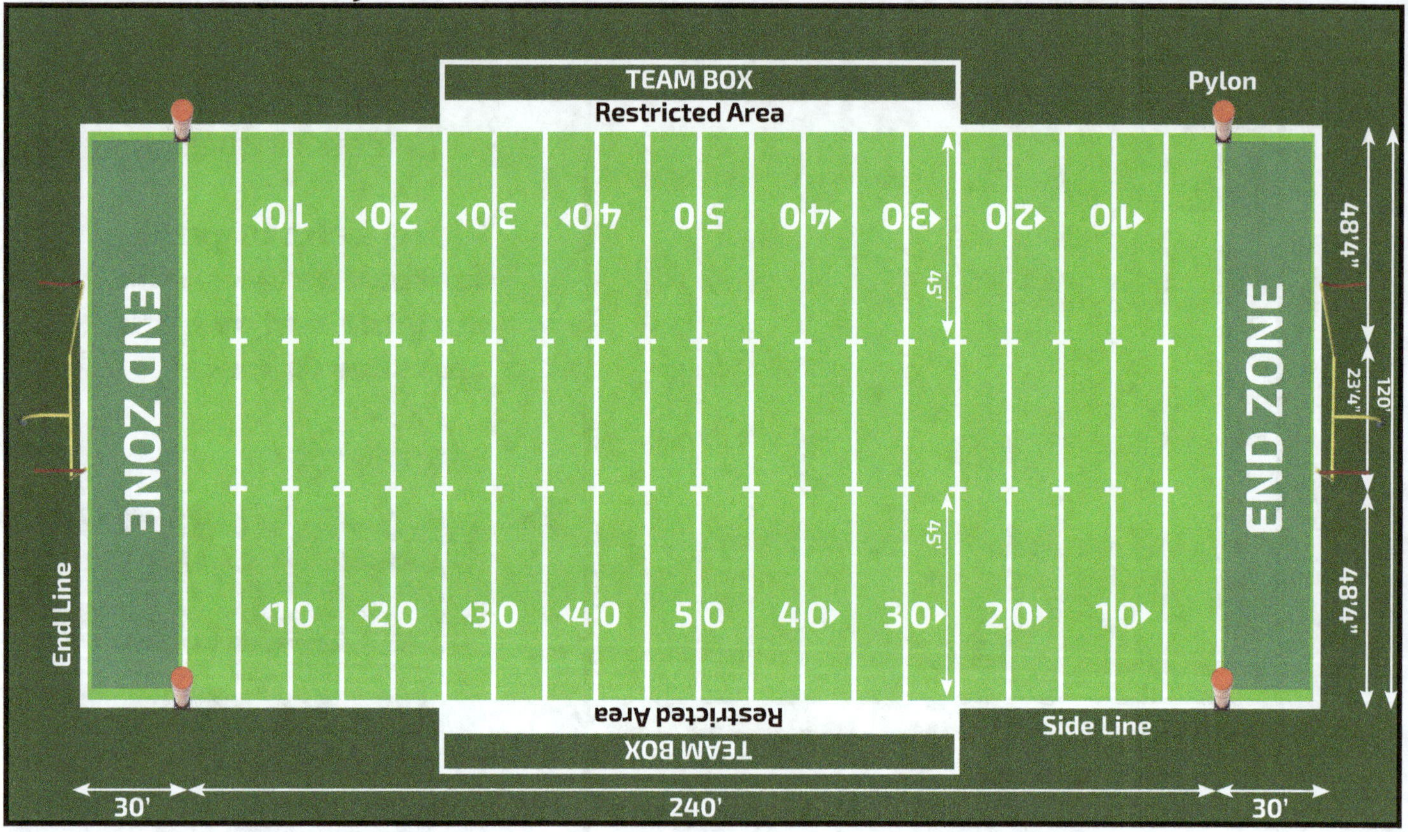

Goalpost Dimensions

Key Parts of the Field

- **End Zones:** These are the scoring areas at each end of the field. When a player reaches the end zone with the ball, that's a touchdown!

- **Goal Lines:** The line that separates the end zone from the rest of the field.

- **50-Yard Line:** The middle of the field—teams switch sides after halftime.

- **Yard Lines:** Marked every 5 yards across the field to show how far teams need to go.

- **Hash Marks:** Small lines on the field that help position the ball before each play.

- **Sidelines:** The long boundary lines along each side of the field.

- **Goalposts:** Located in the back of each end zone and used for kicking field goals or extra points.

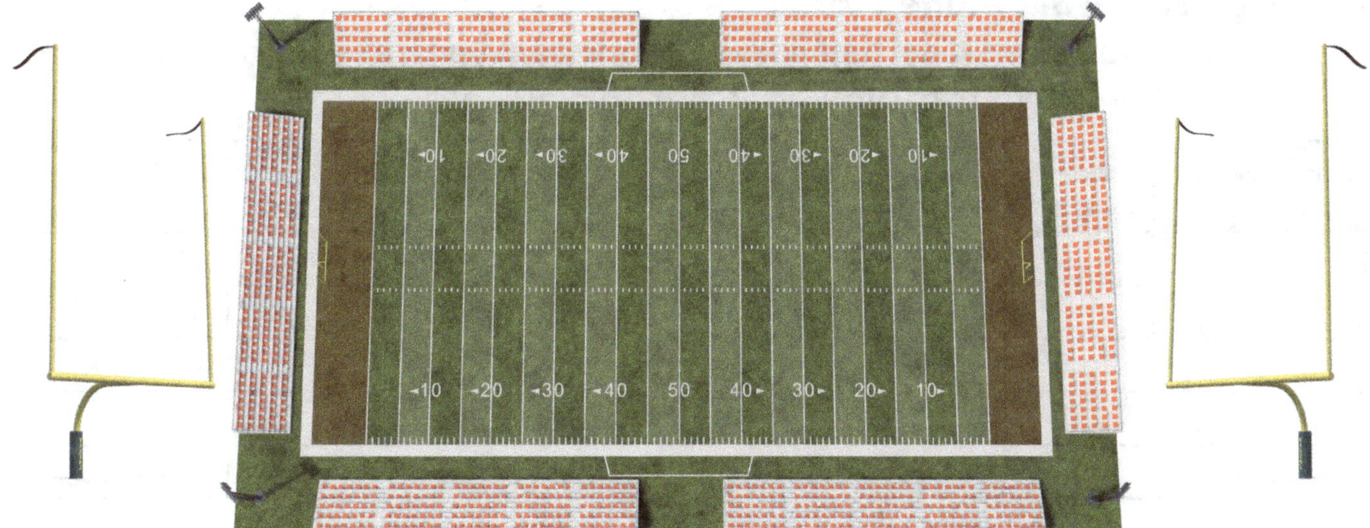

Football Stats Activity Page: "Be the Coach!"

What Are Stats?

Stats (short for statistics) help us understand what's happening in the game. Coaches and players use stats to see how well they're doing!

Here are a few simple ones you can track:

Touchdowns (TDs) -How many times a team scores by reaching the end zone (6 points).

Passes Completed-How many times a quarterback throws and a teammate catches the ball.

Yards Gained-How far the ball moves forward during a play.

Tackles Made -How many times a player stops someone with the ball.

Activity: Track Your Game Stats!

Instructions: Play a mini football game in your backyard, at school, or at recess. Use the chart below to track your stats while playing!

Player Name	Touchdowns	Passes Completed	Yards Gained	Tackles Made	Sacks
1					
2					
3					
4					
5					

Fun Game: Stat Toss!

Supplies:
A football, paper, pencil, and cones or markers for distance.

Set up:

1. Place 3 cones at different distances:
   Cone 1 = 5 yards
   Cone 2 = 10 yards
   Cone 3 = 15 yards

2. Throw the ball and record where it lands.

Scoring:

- Cone 1 = 5 yards gained

- Cone 2 = 10 yards gained

- Cone 3 = 15 yards gained

Throw	1	2	3	4	5	Total Yards

- **Stat Talk!**

After you fill out your stats, ask:

- Who got the most touchdowns?

- Who had the most tackles?

- What was the total number of yards gained by your whole team?

Football Hall of Fame Scrapbook

Cut out pictures of your favorite players or teams and glue them here. Or draw them yourself!

Who is your favorite football player and why?

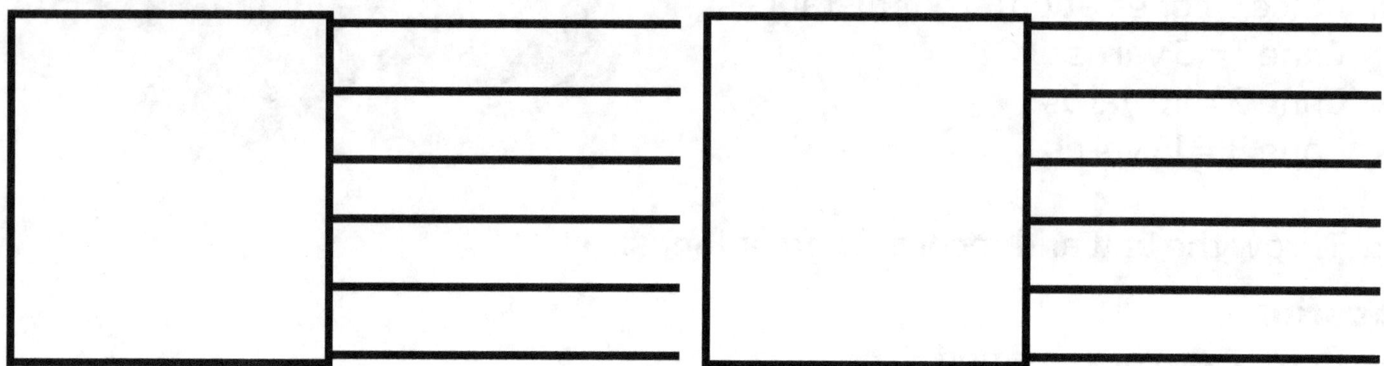

Football Hall of Fame Scrapbook

Try these moves in your backyard or at recess! Check off each one when you complete it:

☐ Spin Move
☐ Juke Move (fake one way, go the other)
☐ Touchdown Dance
☐ Hurdle (pretend safely!)
☐ Stiff Arm (practice the motion, not actual contact)

Football Quiz Time!

Circle the correct answer

1. How many players are on the field for one team?
    a) 9
    b) 11
    c) 15
2. What is it called when a player scores in the end zone?
    a) Field goal
    b) Slam dunk
    c) Touchdown
3. What do we call it when a quarterback gets tackled behind the line?
    a) Fumble
    b) Interception
    c) Sack

Match the Player to the Position!

Draw a line from the position to what they do:

Position	What They Do
Quarterback	A. Tries to catch passes and run fast
Wide Receiver	B. Kicks field goals
Running Back	C. Runs with the ball after handoffs
Kicker	D. Throws the football
Linebacker	E. Stops the other team from scoring

Answer Key: 1-D, 2-A, 3-C, 4-B, 5-E

Conclusion

Football is a fantastic sport that anyone can play and enjoy! Whether you're playing for fun, joining a team, or dreaming of becoming a pro, football helps you stay active, make friends, and learn teamwork. Now that you know the rules, strategies, and cool moves, grab a football and start playing!

Football Quiz Time!

Circle the correct answer

1. **How many players are on the field for one team?**
   a) 9
   b) 11
   c) 15
2. **What is it called when a player scores in the end zone?**
   a) Field goal
   b) Slam dunk
   c) Touchdown
3. **What do we call it when a quarterback gets tackled behind the line?**
   a) Fumble
   b) Interception
   c) Sack

Match the Player to the Position!

Draw a line from the position to what they do:

Position	What They Do
Quarterback	A. Tries to catch passes and run fast
Wide Receiver	B. Kicks field goals
Running Back	C. Runs with the ball after handoffs
Kicker	D. Throws the football
Linebacker	E. Stops the other team from scoring

Conclusion

Football is a fantastic sport that anyone can play and enjoy! Whether you're playing for fun, joining a team, or dreaming of becoming a pro, football helps you stay active, make friends, and learn teamwork. Now that you know the rules, strategies, and cool moves, grab a football and start playing!

- **Quarterback** – The leader of the offense who throws or hands off the ball.

- **Touchdown** – Scoring by getting the ball into the end zone.

- **Interception** – When the defense catches a pass meant for the offense.

- **Fumble** – Losing the ball during a play.

- **Sack** – Tackling the quarterback behind the line of scrimmage.

- **Huddle** – When players gather to plan their next play.

Happy playing!

Glossary

Design Your Own Football Jersey

Instructions:

Draw a jersey for your dream football team! Choose your team name, favorite number, and team colors. Don't forget to add a logo!

Think About:

What animal or symbol could represent your team?
What colors make your team stand out?

Design Your Own Football Jersey

Design Your Own Football Jersey

Design Your Own Football Jersey

AMAZON STORE
YOUTUBE SUBSCRIBE
PLAYFUL PLANET KIDS SHOW
ROCK-IT

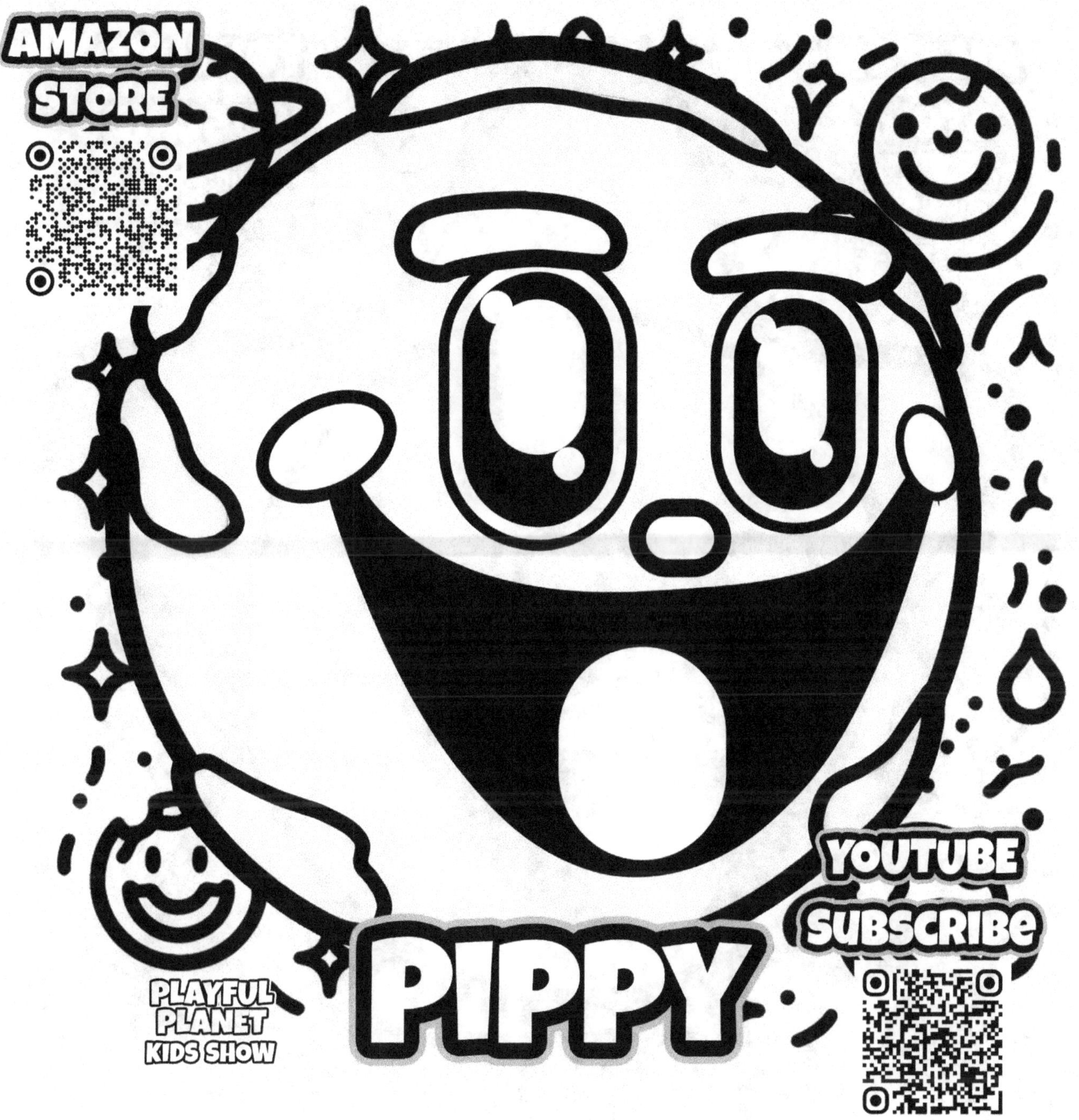

AMAZON
STORE
PLAYFUL
PLANET
KIDS SHOW
PIPPY
YOUTUBE
SUBSCRIBE

AMAZON STORE
YOUTUBE SUBSCRIBE
PLAYFUL PLANET KIDS SHOW
STARSHINE

AMAZON STORE
YOUTUBE
PLAYFUL PLANET KIDS SHOW
SUBSCRIBE
ASTROID

AMAZON STORE
YOUTUBE
SUBSCRIBE
PLAYFUL PLANET KIDS SHOW
SUNNY

PLANET
KIDS SHOW
AMAZON
STORE
YOUTUBE
SUBSCRIBE
LUNAR

PLAYFUL PLANET
KIDS SHOW
AMAZON
STORE
YOUTUBE
SUBSCRIBE

CERTIFICATE OF COMPLETION.

THIS CERTIFICATE IS PRESENTED

GREAT JOB!

DATE

PLAYFUL
PLANET
KIDS SHOW

Parents and caregivers are invited to watch alongside their little ones. We encourage you to actively participate, imitate sounds, and engage in the activities shown on the screen to enhance your child's learning and development.

Welcome to **[Preschool with Pippy]**, where the magic of reading and writing begins!
At **age 3**, your child is embarking on an exciting journey of literacy development. By now, they should be showing signs of readiness for reading and writing, including:

- **Language Skills:** Your child may be using more complex sentences and expanding their vocabulary daily. They may also enjoy rhymes, songs, and storytelling.

- **Print Awareness:** Look for signs that your child recognizes letters and numbers in their environment, such as on signs, labels, and books. They may also be interested in scribbling and drawing, demonstrating an early understanding of writing.

- **Interest in Books:** Encourage your child's love for books by reading together regularly. They may enjoy simple stories with colorful illustrations and may even begin to "read" familiar books by memory.

- **Fine Motor Skills:** Developing fine motor skills is crucial for writing readiness. Activities such as drawing, coloring, and tracing lines can help strengthen these skills.

- **Curiosity and Engagement:** Your child's curiosity about the world around them is blossoming. Encourage their natural curiosity by providing opportunities for exploration and hands-on learning experiences.

As you read and explore The preschool with Pippy Series together, remember to celebrate your child's progress and enjoy this special time of growth and discovery.

Happy reading!

Playful Planet Kids Show.